P9-ECZ-854

Ancient Israel after Catastrophe

The Religious World View of the Mishnah

Ancient Israel after Catastrophe

The Religious World View of the Mishnah

JACOB NEUSNER

University Press of Virginia
Charlottesville

The Richard Lectures for 1981–82
University of Virginia
THE UNIVERSITY PRESS OF VIRGINIA

First published 1983
Printed in the United States of America

Library of Congress Cataloging in Publication Data

Neusner, Jacob, 1932 -
Ancient Israel after catastrophe.

(Richard lectures)
Includes index.
1. Mishnah—Theology. 2. Judaism—History—Talmudic
period, 10-425. I. Title. II. Series.
BM497.8.N472 1983 296.1'2306 82-15972
ISBN 0-8139-0980-5

For Allen Fitchen

CONTENTS

Preface

The Richard Lectures, which I have the honor to present for 1981–82, are meant to engage the interest of a broad academic audience, including students. Since my theme is surviving calamity, I believe I meet the conditions of the invitation. The fundamental human experience to which I devote these lectures seems particularly appropriate to the setting and constituency of the University of Virginia. For I speak of defeat and the experience of reconstruction, of the aftermath of a hopeless war and the response of the intellectuals among the survivors. It is appropriate, too, for me as a Jew to take up the issues of defeat and survival. For, in the nature of things, we Jews look out upon the world just passed as upon an abyss. We stand on the other side of that abyss. The South, in losing, retained its society, its land, and its hope for a future for all Southerners, now happily coming to fulfillment. But we who lost so many millions in death factories in the recent war no longer imagine the possibility of restoring the world that was lost, any more than we shall ever see the five million men and women, and the million children, our families, who were murdered.

Yet if truth be told, among humanity at large, what people are not survivors? And to whom are not pertinent the lessons of how to endure defeat? In the book of human history how many pages have been written by the defeated: the Incas, Mayas, Aztecs; the Poles,

Afghanis, Kurds; Albanians, Serbo-Croatians, and Montenegrans; Germans, Japanese; the Narragansett, Iroquois; Frieslanders and Gronings; Scots, Welsh, and Irish; Basques and Catalans—not to mention the South then and the Jews of then and now. The list of victorious empires of times past yet with us today is not a very long one; I cannot think of any winners of two hundred years ago still vigorous and important upon the world stage, except for us and the Russians. But the losers—that is a long list indeed. Nearly all of them survived—by definition—and survive today as conquered provinces of mind. That, then, is what we should want to know if we ask about what is interesting to a broad audience, I mean, a human experience awaiting analysis and demanding attention. What does it mean to lose and yet survive?

We must remind ourselves, moreover, that the generality of Americans—not Jews, not Southerners—today know the inner stress of national loss. When our country suffered defeat in Vietnam, all Americans entered the experience of Virginia and of the South. It is appropriate therefore to reflect in this place, at this time, on the themes of defeat and reconstruction, chaos and the reordering of society, pollution and the restoration of the holy. In listing these topics, I refer to the formative experiences of that kind of Judaism deemed definitive from the first and second centuries to the present day. As I shall explain, the first document of Judaism as we know it is the Mishnah, a utopian design for the sacred society formed by Israel, the Jewish people in the Land of Israel. The Mishnah reached closure toward the end of the second century and is a document of the later first and second centuries. Since in that time the Jews were defeated in two great wars against the Romans, losing their autonomous government, their holy Temple, their mode of worship of God and organizing a holy society alike, we confront a document of a people in their hour of defeat. What you already realize is that, in those terrible times, the defeated Israelites framed a vision and conceived of a system to withstand whatever time would bring. From their day to our own, what they planted has flourished. So the sages who framed the Mishnah perceived and perpetuated an enduring vision. But the world on which they gazed revealed to their eyes only ruins. The Mishnah is the insight of their inner eye, a vision beyond catastrophe. We who have yet to reflect deeply on the shame of our nation's defeat may learn about the tasks beyond as we consider the program of these visionaries beyond defeat, dreamers on the other side of the abyss.

To conclude: Here we reflect upon the experience of passage from high hope to bitter disappointment. I speak of a world at the end of an old and long-established order and the beginning of an age lacking all precedent, all points of reference and orientation. These lectures are about losers, people who lost the world they and their ancestors had always known. But the losers also were survivors. This is one instance of how humanity responds to life lacking compass, all center and sense, how people live in a world that has lost its moorings. For when old landmarks crumbled and were swept away, second-century Israel made new maps and set out new markers, through an act of surpassing will. The Mishnah is their record. My conviction, therefore, is that the human experience captured by a very odd and remote document addresses issues both immediate and illuminating.

This book is dedicated to a friend and co-worker who, different from me in all ways but the ones that matter, shares with me a common sensibility, intellectual judgment, and taste. Having been discovered, at last, after publishing about a hundred books, I found in Allen Fitchen that editor able both to win my perfect confidence and to gain ample confidence in me. The result is that, between the two of us and among our friends, we aim to do something memorable in our shared fields of bringing important books into the world (Fitchen) about the accessible, human experience of the Jewish people (Neusner). It is a privilege to offer to him these lectures as a token of esteem and thanks.

I have the happy duty, finally, to thank the Committee for the Richard Lectures for the honor of inviting me to give these lectures, and Professor William H. Harbaugh, Commonwealth Professor of History and Chairman of the committee, for his cordial management of the details, beginning to end. I thank also those colleagues and new friends at the University of Virginia who extended hospitality during my visit in Charlottesville on April 26–28, 1982.

Providence, Rhode Island
January 25, 1982
1 Shebat 5742

CHAPTER ONE

Reconstruction in an Age of Defeat

i. Why Context Is Critical

The problem of defining the historical context in which the Mishnah came into being demands considerable attention at the outset. Once that context is clear, the salient traits of the document will take on more than formal interest. The route to interpreting the Mishnah and its social meaning lies through describing where it came into being. For the beginning of interpretation is to relate history to ideas, context to content. So we start with historical context.

The labor of describing the context is especially important in the case of the Mishnah, for the Mishnah, as a utopian law code, tells us nothing about the world it proposes to address. It faces inward, partitioned off from the world by blank and opaque walls. Accordingly, there is no point of entry. To begin with, when the Mishnah speaks, where are we as listeners supposed to be located? Indeed, falling into the hands of someone who has never seen it, the Mishnah must cause puzzlement. From the first line to the last, discourse takes up questions internal to a system that is never introduced. The Mishnah provides information without establishing context. It presents disputes about facts hardly urgent outside of a circle of faceless disputants, who are nowhere in particular. Consequently, we start with the impression that we join a conversation already long under way about topics we can never grasp anyhow. Even though the language is our own, the substance is not. We shall feel as if we are in a transit lounge at a distant airport. We hear announcements and understand the words people say. But we are baffled by their meanings and concerns, above all, by the urgency in their voices: What are you telling me? Why must I know it? Who cares if I do not? As with Cockney or Strine, this language we speak in common is made strange.

Before us is a remarkable statement of concerns for matters not only wholly remote from our own world but, in the main, alien to the world of the people who made the Mishnah itself. It is as if people sat down to write letters about things they had never seen, to people they did not know—letters from an unknown city to an undefined and unimagined world: the Mishnah is from no one special, in a far utopia, to whom it may concern.

ii. Why the Mishnah Is Important

The Mishnah is a law code, made about A.D. 200, out of legal traditions extending back for approximately two centuries. It is in six parts or divisions, covering laws pertinent to agriculture, the calendar's sacred times and seasons, family life with special reference to women, civil law and institutions, the everyday conduct of the Temple sacrificial cult, and the purity laws governing access to the Temple and to other holy or priestly foods. This brief description raises in startling form the simple question: Why should anyone want to know about such a document? It would be difficult to identify a set of rules less relevant to our own day and age than the ones under extended discussion in this book.

Accordingly, before we know what the Mishnah is, we shall want to ask why it is important to know what it is. The answer to that question leaps out of the simple equation that follows:

<table>
<tr><td>Old Testament</td><td rowspan="2">=</td><td>Written Torah
(Hebrew Scriptures)</td></tr>
<tr><td>New Testament</td><td>Oral Torah (Mishnah
and its continuators)</td></tr>
</table>

The equation would speak more eloquently if you knew what is meant by the elements on the right side of it. The top line on both sides speaks of the same holy book, but with the words particular to Christianity and Judaism, respectively. That is to say, the biblical books that Christians know as "the Old Testament," Judaism knows as the Written Torah. Clearly, in both religious traditions, the reason is that there is another holy book complementing and completing the Hebrew Scriptures. In the former case, as everyone knows, it is the New Testament. In the latter, as only a few people realize, it is the Oral Torah. The principal myth of Judaism is that when Moses ascended to Mount Sinai, God revealed to him two Torahs, which, together, constitute "the one whole Torah" of Moses. One of the two was in writing. The other was formulated and transmitted, not in writing, but orally and through memorization. The Mishnah is the first and principal expression of this other Torah, the Oral Torah revealed to Moses at Sinai. All of the books of Judaism produced beyond the Mishnah, in particular, the Talmuds of the Land of Israel and of Babylonia, rest upon the Mishnah and so constitute parts of that Oral Torah. So far I have explained why it is important to know what the Mishnah is. The reason is that the Mishnah constitutes the first document of the form of Judaism that has predominated from the time of the Mishnah to our own day, replacing all that had gone before, absorbing all that would come afterward, into a single mythic structure and legal-religious system.

But we still know nothing at all about the Mishnah. For, as soon as the document comes into view, the things said *about* it become less interesting (let alone credible) than the things *it* says, that is, the world view which it expresses. The bulk of these lectures is an effort to describe the world view, explaining how it took shape, its principal stimuli, sources, and emphases, and what it meant to the people who made it up: how the Mishnah spoke to Israel beyond catastrophe. So it would not serve to attempt in a few words to say what will take a great many anyhow. What you have to know at this point are a few very simple facts.

First, the Mishnah is a law code in the sense that it contains statements about things we should do and not do.

Second, the Mishnah is a book of religion in the sense that it speaks in large part about religious things, holy days, deeds, duties, holiness and how we become holy.

Third, the Mishnah is systematic and orderly, presenting a complete and cogent statement, a world view and way of life—in context, a Judaism.

Whether or not the world of its day conformed to its system, the system itself is what matters. That is how we find our way into the imagination and sensibility of the framers of the document. What counts is their consciousness and conscience. In the end what we want to know is how those men solved the problem of their day, because, as I said, it has turned out to be a perennial and painful problem long afterward, and not only for Israel. How to recover order when everything seems disorderly, how to build when the ground beneath is trembling, how to look forward when there is little reason to—this is what they reckoned to do.

iii. The Mishnah as Enigma

The Mishnah does not identify its authors. In its authorities' patterns of language and speech, it permits only slight variations, so there is no place for individual characteristics of expression. It does not tell us when it speaks. It does not address a particular place or time. It rarely speaks of events in its own day. It never identifies its prospective audience. There is scarcely a "you" of direct address to the reader in the entire mass of sayings and rules. The Mishnah begins nowhere: "When do we do so and so?" It ends abruptly. There is no predicting where it will commence, no explaining why it is done. Where, when, why the document is laid out and set forth are questions not deemed urgent.

Indeed, the Mishnah contains not a hint about what its authors conceive their work to be. Is it a law code? Is it a schoolbook? Since it makes statements describing what people should and should not do, or rather, do do and do not do, we might suppose it is a law code. Since, as we shall see later on, it covers topics of both practical and theoretical interest, we might suppose it is a schoolbook, a work of philosophy. But the Mishnah never expresses a hint about its authors' intent. The reason is that the authors do what they must to efface all traces not only of individuality but even of their own participation in the formation of the document.

So it is not only a letter from utopia to whom it may concern. It also is a letter written by no one person—but not by a committee, either. If, then, we turn to the contents of the document, we are helped not at all in determining the place of the Mishnah's origin, the purpose of its making, the reasons for its anonymous and collective plane of discourse and monotonous tone of voice. The Mishnah covers a carefully defined program of topics, as I shall explain presently. But the Mishnah never tells us why one topic is introduced and another is omitted, or what the agglutination of these particular topics is meant to accomplish in the formation of a system or of an imaginative construction. Nor is there any predicting how a given topic will be treated, why a given set of issues will be explored in close detail, and another set of possible issues ignored. Discourse on a theme begins and ends as if all things are self-evident—including, as I said, the reason for beginning at one point and ending at some other.

In all, one might readily imagine, upon first glance at this strange and curious book, that what we have is a rulebook. It appears on the surface to be a book lacking all traces of eloquence and style, revealing no evidence of system and reflection, serving no important purpose. First glance indicates that what we have in hand is yet another shard from remote antiquity—no different from the lists of kings inscribed on ancient shards, the random catalogue of (to us) useless, meaningless facts: a cookbook, a placard of posted tariffs, detritus of random information accidentally thrown up on the currents of historical time. Who would want to have made such a thing? Who would now want to refer to it?

We shall be a long time in answering these questions. First, let us ask for that information we, in our place and time, think definitive. What was happening in the time and place in which the Mishnah was made, I mean, in the first and second centuries, among the Israelites (as the Jews of the country refer to themselves in their writings) who lived in the Land of Israel (as they called the Holy Land)?

iv. Age of Hope and Despair

First-century Jews in the Land of Israel looked for a messiah, expected any day. They undertook great and terrible wars in their quest. Defeated once and for all at the end of the first third of the second century, in 135, the Jews found little reason to hope for a messiah any more. In the aftermath of crushing defeat, it is difficult to know what anyone was willing to do. The first century was a time of high hope and courageous deed. The second century was an age of disillusion and despair. In the first century people fought wars. In the second a few—the authorities of the Mishnah—made plans and dreamed dreams. In the first century Israel's messiahs and their warriors produced disaster. In the second Israel's sages wrote a book. The Jewish nation went from doing things to imagining systems, like the second-century gnostics, from active deeds of history to dreams and fantasies about a future tightly held in the hands of God.

Let me expand on this point. The first century for the Jewish nation was a time of concrete action in the real, material world of sword and blood. The second century was an age of system-building, making things up in the mind, spinning a web of reality out of the gossamer threads of attenuated hope. It was a time of philosophy, inner reconstruction. The first century called forth politicians, generals, holy men and heroes—doers all. The second demanded those who could conceive life beyond despair, imagine utopia, and make laws about constructing it here and now—dreamers all. The first century drew to its close—effectively, at the end of Bar Kokhba's war—with the Jewish people glutting the slave markets, the southern part of their land in ruins, villages and farms up for grabs. The world had not been saved by a messiah but ruined by whatever messiahs Israel had followed. The second century came to an end—

effectively, with the formation of the Mishnah, some time around A.D. 200—with the Jews in the land enjoying limited self-government under a Roman client-ruler of their own people, living at peace in their farming villages, contending with the leadership of leading men who brought renewal and inaugurated a protracted age of reconstruction. Generals had destroyed. Men of learning (there was scarcely a woman among the sages, and none by the end of the second century) now built. Messiahs had projected a history and promised to conclude it. Sages spoke of what was permanent and on-going, made the end of history depend upon doing what exactly they said—hence, in the nature of things, postponing it, really, forever. First-century Israel had spoken of time and end-time. Second-century Israel now built eternity.

It was only the disaster of severe, irreversible defeats that succeeded in driving from the proscenium of Israelite consciousness people who made promises and tried to keep them. The end of the old order alone won the nation's attention for the quiet people, philosophers and lawyers, who insisted on much and promised little. The first century looked for change and made history. The second century dreamed of permanence and avoided history. Its legacy is a set of laws, governing and describing how things are or should be. Its message to us is a tale of order. It promises an account of predictable, reliable things, speaking of a world at rest. It describes the pattern of a society aiming at perfection and sanctification, just as, when things were very good at the beginning, God had sanctified it all. And when all things had come to rest, there would be no history at all. The gift of the first century is the example of courage and martyrdom on the battlefield. The enduring endowment of the second century is the lesson of building a holy people and the law for living the holy life called Judaism. That is why we can speak of events of the first century down to 135, but only the ideas of the second to 200. We may describe the history made in the first century, but only the vision of eternity—lawful, unchanging life, posited by the philosophers of the second.

Rapidly, and in general terms, let me review the principal events in Judaism in the two centuries. There are only three: (1) the first war against Rome, from 66 to 73, with its climax in August 70, in the destruction of the Temple of Jerusalem, the abrogation of its sacrificial order, the burning of the city, and the capture and slaughter, or enslavement, of masses of people; (2) the second war against Rome, from 132 to 135, with its still greater human disaster and its aftermath of brief repression and the permanent closing off of Jerusalem from Jewish access; and (3) the formation of the Mishnah and its adoption as the constitution and law code of the Jewish government of the Land of Israel toward the year 200. These are the three events—two wars and a book—that set the boundaries around the period in which the Judaism before us took shape, in the very forms in which we have known Judaism from that time to this.

To speak of each war briefly: (1) in the first century, as I said, a great many Jews in the Land of Israel looked for and expected a messiah. Whether he would be a wonder-worker, magician, teacher of righteousness, a general, a God-man, hope for his coming provoked people to vigorous action. Some left their homes and families and followed a messiah. Others joined together in military or monastic bands. For all it was a time to do things in the belief that history had approached its climax and reached its end. So there were things to be done to get ready for the end. But, as we now know, what they did was validate the expectation of the end, for it really was the end of the world as anyone had known it.

(2) In the earlier part of the second century, these same hopes for God's intervention in the life of Israel in its land came to a crescendo in the war led by Ben Kosibah, whom some called Bar Kokhba, son of a star. The aftermath of the calamity of that last messianic war for the Jews of the Holy Land in ancient times proved to be a defeat of more than this-worldly proportions. For the Jews of the land lost not only a war. Gone for good were the Temple and its ongoing life of celebration, service to God, animal offerings, and other rites concretely to link Israel to God enthroned on high. Since the Temple had flourished, with a brief interruption, for more than eleven hundred years, we cannot but stand in awe at the change that then proved to be final.

v. The Center and the Pivot: The Temple

To understand the gravity of the change, we recall that for eleven centuries and more, the Jewish people had organized its entire life—social, metaphysical, natural and super-natural—around sacrifice organized in the Jerusalem Temple. The cult had marked off the passage of time and the seasons through the punctuation of slaughtering sacrifices of sheep and cows. Israel had recognized the hierarchy of its society by reference to priests and Levites, then Israelites. Three times a year all Israelites were supposed to come to Jerusalem; many did at least once a year. These climactic moments, marking the passage of the natural year and celebrating the formative moments in Israel's national life with God as well, infused the Israelites' life with meaning, made sense of nation and nature all at once. Nor should we forget that, in ancient times, meat generally was eaten in a cultic setting, as part of a meal served to God and shared with God. Consequently, these massive gatherings in Jerusalem, with their exalted moments of celebration and their outpourings of petition, their thanks for what God had given and their beseeching for what God now must give, the processions and parades, with their bonfires and their barbecues—these defined the order of life. In the Temple in Jerusalem, Israel celebrated God and creation, humanity and the nation, and also ate heartily and well. What was left of the calendar that had marked off the passage of seasons as sacred, had linked the spatial arrangements of the world with the cosmic order of the moon and the passage of time, after 135 was mere memory. With its system of celebration and cult permanently in ruins, all that Israel had was the memory of the celebration and the hope for the restoration of the cult. But memories melt, and hope, postponed of realization, scarcely sustains forever.

Ancient Israel, in the first and second centuries, discovered how to confront and overcome the end of everything that mattered. The critical point came in the second century, as I said, with the final and conclusive catastrophe: the Temple site plowed over, Jerusalem barred to Jews, the entire way of celebrating creation and living by revelation and aiming at redemption a mass of broken blocks and sealed-off ruins. For within one generation the foundations had been laid for Judaism as we know it, that is, the religion which Jews have kept and which has kept them for the rest of their history to the present day. It was a way for losers and survivors, remarkably appropriate to their condition then, unhappily congruent to the condition of humanity then and now. We had best listen to anyone who can teach us how to hope and not despair.

vi. Guilt and Sin, Atonement and Reconciliation

The Temple stood at the very center of the order of Israelite society. It also filled the heart of Israel. For from ancient times Israelites had held that, if they sinned, the way to atone was to bring a sacrifice. True, the prophets had also emphasized the need for loyalty and sincere repentence. No one by the first century could have imagined that you could trade a goat for a deliberate act of adultery or murder. Still, the Temple in its day served as a means of atoning for sin, and the sacrifice effected the removal of guilt.

The cult was a principal means of atonement and reconciliation with God. The personal and psychological importance of the cult, moreover, found a counterpart in the national and social meaning assigned to it. We recall that, when the first Temple was destroyed in 586 B.C., various prophets had interpreted the destruction as a mode of divine punishment for Israel's sin. When, about three generations later, it was rebuilt, the conviction that Israel had been reconciled with God grew firm. Israelite history for the period before 586 was rewritten in terms of sin and punishment, leading to destruction, then suffering and atonement, leading to reconciliation—the whole of history embodied in the story of the Temple building and sacrifices. So the books of Joshua, Judges, Samuel, and Kings presented a new history for old Israel.

When the Temple was destroyed in A.D. 70, it was perfectly natural, therefore, to interpret the event as a penalty for sin. To be sure, various parties to the event had their own ideas about what that sin had been. The Christians said the Temple had been destroyed because of the failure of Israel of that time to become Christian. The Romans regarded it as self-evident that the Temple had been destroyed because the Jews had rebelled against Roman rule. Within Israel itself, there were some who accused the priests of conducting the affairs of the Temple in a less than punctilious manner. Yet the biblical paradigm remained to help people endure the awful event. For, as before, in about three generations, after much suffering, Israel would expiate whatever sins had brought about its calamity, and the Temple would be recovered and rebuilt. Whether that is why the messianic war led by Ben Kosiba enjoyed the massive national support it apparently had we do not know; it is a commonly held view.

We do know that in the aftermath of Ben Kosiba's defeat, with Jerusalem closed to Jews and the Temple site plowed over, no one could have retained the illusion that the biblical pattern once more would be repeated.

Now in paying attention to the social crisis of Israel in the aftermath of permanent defeat, we must not ignore the inner disaster. The consciousness of guilt for the destruction of the Temple, a point on which the biblical heritage harped, becomes acute beyond all bearing when joined to a second matter. Without Temple and cult for the expiation of guilt, where could people turn? Israelites faced an impasse; they confessed sin but had no means of atoning it, felt guilt but lacked remission, sought atonement but had lost all access to the place and mode of reconciliation. Israel in the second century faced a different sort of defeat from the South in 1865. While the South retained its fundamental social strength and institutions, in time even framing a common ideal for all of its people and the nation as a whole, it also possessed the foundations for future construction. Second-century Israel, by contrast, lost the social framework of the nation, beyond the simplest social organism represented by the village and the components thereof. The South emerged from its tragic war pride and self-respect intact. Israel blamed itself for what had happened, and the entire heritage of its past stood as judge and prosecutor in testifying against that generation. What was left of the heart and soul on which once more to build a nation?

vii. Conclusion

Judaism in its first two centuries came into being on the other side of two wars and produced, as its first and enduring testimony, a book of law and religion, a book to express a system of philosophy and a theory of society. Since the Mishnah emerges after a time of wars, the one thing we should anticipate is a message about the meaning of history, an account of events and their meaning. Central to the Mishnah's system should be a picture of the course of Israel's destiny, in the tradition of the biblical histories—Samuel, Kings, Chronicles, for instance—and in the tradition of the prophets of ancient Israel, the several Isaiahs, Jeremiah, and the rest.

The Mishnah's principal insistence is the opposite. It speaks of what is permanent and enduring: the flow of time through the seasons, marked by festivals and sabbaths; the procedures of the cult through the regular and enduring sacrifices; the conduct of the civil society through norms of fairness to prevent unjust change; the pursuit of agricultural work in accord with the rules of holiness; the enduring, unchanging invisible phobias of cultic uncleanness and cleanness. In the Mishnah there is no division devoted to the interpretation of history. There is no pretense even at telling what had just happened.

There is scarcely a line to address the issue of the meaning of the disasters of the day.

The Mishnah does not address onetime events of history. Its laws express recurrent patterns, eternal patterns as enduring as the movement of the moon and sun around the earth (as they would have understood it) and as regular as the lapping of the waves on the beach. These are laws on plowing, planting, harvesting; birth, marriage, procreation, death; home, family, household; work, rest; sunrise, sunset—not the stuff of history. The laws speak of the here and now, not of state and tradition, past or future. Since, when the ideas of the Mishnah took shape, most other Jews expressed a keen interest in history, the contrast cannot be missed. The Mishnah imagines a world of regularity and order in the aftermath of the end of ancient certainties and patterns. It designs laws after the old rules all were broken or had fallen into desuetude. It speaks of an eternal present—generally using the continuous present tense and describing how things are—to people beyond all touch with their own past, its life and institutions. Its message, then, is clear.

CHAPTER TWO

Stability in an Age of Disorder

i. Reaction and Reactionism

The response of intellectuals to catastrophe is hardly to be described on the basis of one example only. But it is worth asking what the thinkers of the Mishnah addressing the age beyond the end exemplify. Let me try to say. If I were asked to predict how educated people might address the world beyond doomsday (for surely some would survive, at least for a time) on the basis of how the sages of the Mishnah spoke to their own time, it would be an account rich in irony. For intellectuals turn out to exhibit contradictory traits. They are profoundly conservative, looking backward for precedents and guidelines. But they innovate in subtle and unselfconscious ways. So their points of innovation take shape within the framework of self-evidence.

That is to say, it is as if to claim whatever new things I do are self-evidently true, so there can be nothing new or strange. Beyond the abyss of calamity, therefore, we find that the most powerful impulse is to speak of the future in terms of the past. The heritage of ancient Israel supplied the guidelines for the

Mishnah's account of future Israel. Accordingly, as we shall see, the Mishnah's utopian plan follows the lines surveyed by ancient priests and adheres so closely, in so many ways, to what had gone before as to suggest the Mishnah offers nothing new. Its affirmation, then, is reactionary: the old order endures, nothing has changed. The irony of which I spoke is contained in that absurd claim. The truth is the opposite. In the Mishnah everything has changed. As I shall explain, even biblical Hebrew is abandoned. Nothing endures. To grasp the irony clearly, let me first indicate the full extent of the programmatic conservatism represented by the Mishnah, simply by telling you its principal interests.

The Mishnah is a six-part code of descriptive rules. The six divisions are: (1) agricultural rules; (2) laws governing appointed seasons, e.g., sabbaths and festivals; (3) laws on the transfer of women and property along with women from one man (father) to another (husband); (4) the system of civil and criminal law (corresponding to what we today should regard as "the legal system"); (5) laws for the conduct of the cult and the Temple; and (6) laws on the preservation of cultic purity both in the Temple and under certain domestic circumstances, with special reference to the table and bed. These divisions define the range and realm of reality.

Since, as we know, in the aftermath of the war against Rome in 132–35, the Temple was declared permanently prohibited to Jews, and Jerusalem was closed off to them as well, the Mishnah's laws in part speak of nowhere and not now. There was no cult, no

Temple, no holy city, to which, at this time, the description of the Mishnaic laws applied. We observe at the very outset, therefore, that a sizable proportion of the Mishnah deals with matters to which the sages had no material access or practical knowledge at the time of their work. They themselves were not members of the priestly caste. Yet we have seen that the Mishnah contains a division on the conduct of the cult, namely, the fifth, as well as one on the conduct of matters so as to preserve the cultic purity of the sacrificial system along the lines laid out in the book of Leviticus, the sixth division. Many of the tractates of the first division, on agriculture, deal with the rations provided for the priests by the Israelite farmers out of the produce of the Holy Land. The interests of the division overall flow from the Levitical taboos on land use and disposition of crops; the whole is an exercise of most acute interest to the priests. A fair part of the second division, on appointed times, takes up the conduct of the cult on special days, such as the sacrifices offered on the Day of Atonement, Passover, and the like. Indeed, what the Mishnah wants to know *about* appointed seasons concerns the cult far more than it does the synagogue, which plays a subordinate role. The fourth division, on civil law, for its part presents an elaborate account of a political structure and system of Israelite self-government based on Temple, priesthood, and monarchy, in tractates Sanhedrin and Makkot, not to mention Shebuot and Horayot. This system speaks of king, priest, Temple, and court. Not the Jews, kings, priests, and judges, but the Romans conducted the government of Israel in the Land of Israel when the second century authorities did their work. So it would appear that well over half of the document before us—the first, second, part of the fourth, fifth, and sixth divisions—speaks of cult, Temple, government, priesthood. As we shall see in the third chapter, moreover, the Mishnah takes up a profoundly priestly and Levitical conception of sanctification as the principal statement on Israel's condition. When we consider that, in the very time in which the authorities before us did their work, the Temple lay in ruins, the city of Jerusalem was prohibited to all Israelites, and the Jewish government and administration that had centered on the Temple and based its authority on the holy life lived there were in ruins, the fantastic character of the Mishnah's address to its own catastrophic day becomes clear. Much of the Mishnah speaks of matters not in being when the Mishnah was created because the Mishnah wishes to make its statement on what really matters.

In the age beyond catastrophe, the problem is to reorder a world off-course and adrift, to gain reorientation for an age in which the sun has come out after night and fog. The Mishnah is a document of imagination and fantasy, describing how things "are" out of the shards and remnants of reality, but, in larger measure, building social being out of beams of hope. The Mishnah tells us something about how things were; it tells us everything about how a small group of men wanted things to be. The document is orderly, repetitious, careful in both language and message. It is small-minded, picayune, obvious, dull, routine—everything its age was not. This is the source of the irony at hand: the Mishnah stands in contrast with the world to which it speaks. Its message is one of small achievements and modest hope. It means to defy a world of large disorders and immodest demands. The heirs of heroes build an unheroic folk in the new and ordinary age. As we shall see in the third lecture, the Mishnah's message is that what little a person is able to do matters in supernatural, cosmic ways. It states that message to an Israelite world that can shape affairs in no important ways and speaks to people who by no means will the way things now are. The Mishnah therefore lays down a practical judgment upon, and in favor of, the imagination and will to reshape reality, regain system, reestablish that order upon which trustworthy existence is to be built. All that survived the calamity was despair—therefore, the will. Israel yet commanded its own will, and that, the Mishnah's sages judged, sufficed for the restoration.

ii. Stability and Scripture

The foundation stone of Israelite society and culture was Scripture, that is, the "Old Testament," received as factual and authoritative. Accordingly, in the search for stability, the quest for a source of certain precedents inevitably led to the Torah, the five books of Moses, and the books of prophecy and wisdom-writings as well. The irony of which I spoke at the outset is again revealed when we consider what the sages of the Mishnah did with Scripture, how they made use of the revelation of Sinai.

On the surface, Scripture plays no role at all, since it is rarely cited in the pages of the Mishnah. But, underneath, Scripture undergirds the whole. The really interesting question is, Which passages of Scripture, and how are they used? The answer is that the sages of the Mishnah do pretty much what they want, bringing their program of reconstruction and stabilization to the disembodied verses of Scripture, so (to shift the metaphor) weaving the whole into a fabric of their own design. They wield an ancient authority to design a "reactionary" world—one of their own invention and creation. They innovated in the name of tradition, that is, Scripture.

Accordingly, the irony is underlined, now in reverse. At the outset we observed that the sages designed a world in which the Temple and its cult stood at the pivot. They reframed a stable and meaningful universe by laying out lines of structure from that center. But they addressed a world lacking all access to that center and pivot. They spoke of a cult in Jerusalem, closed to Jews. The very site of the ancient Temple had been plowed over. So the sages described perfection to people lacking all material means to attain it. Now, on the other side, we find the sages utilizing Scripture without saying so, reaffirming the biblical heritage along lines of their own choosing. Once more we perceive a striking disjuncture between what they did and the form in which they did it. A stable society built upon and over an abyss here is matched. Free-wheeling, highly selective use of the authoritative heritage of the past hardly characterizes reactionaries, but innovators. Let me now unpack this second irony.

First, to place the Mishnah into its larger Israelite context, the generality of Israelite theologians and philosophers (if we may use these terms anachronistically), in the centuries between the formation of books of Holy Scripture and then the formation of the canon as a whole, linked themselves to Scripture in one of four ways. First, they imitated the language of the Hebrew Bible, as in the case of the Dead Sea Scrolls. Second, they attributed sayings, whole books, to biblical heroes, signing the names of prophets or holy men, as in the case of the writers of the pseudepigrapha of the Hebrew Bible. Third, they claimed even a fresh encounter with God, a new revelation in line with the old. Fourth, at the very least, there was constant reference to, and citation of, verses of the Hebrew Scripture, as in the case of the Israelite followers of Jesus, Matthew, Mark, and Luke. (Later continuators of the sages of the Mishnah would choose this last way and cite verses of Scripture to prove their propositions.)

So far as I know, the Mishnah is the first book written by Israelites in the Land of Israel that fails to articulate its own linkage to the revelation of Sinai. (In making that statement, I exclude reference to Abot, which is to be treated in its own terms. It is formally unrelated to the rest of the Mishnah.) While the Mishnah clearly addresses Israel, the Jewish people, it is remarkably indifferent to the Hebrew Scriptures. That is to say, the Mishnah makes no effort at imitating the Hebrew of the Hebrew Bible, as do the writers of the Dead Sea Scrolls. The Mishnah does not attribute its sayings to biblical heroes, prophets, or holy men, as do the writings of the pseudonymous authors in the pseudepigrapha of the Hebrew Scriptures. The Mishnah does not claim to emerge from a fresh encounter with God through revelation, as is not uncommon in Israelite writings of the preceding four hundred years; the Holy Spirit is not alleged to speak here. As I said, the sages of the Mishnah rarely cite Scriptures. So all the devices by which other Israelite writers gain credence for their messages are ignored. Perhaps the authority of the Mishnah was self-evident to its authors. But, self-evident or not, they in no way take the trouble to explain to their document's audience why in the name of God people should conform to the descriptive statements contained in their holy book.

So, superficially, the Mishnah is totally indifferent to Scripture. That impression, moreover, is reinforced by the traits of the language of the Mishnah, as I shall suggest in the next section. The framers of Mishnaic discourse, amazingly, never attempt to imitate the language of Scripture, as do those of the Essene writings at Khirbat Qumram. The very redactional structure of Scripture, found to be serviceable to the writer of the Temple scroll, remarkably, is of no interest whatever to the organizers of the Mishnah and its tractates, except in a very few cases (Leviticus 16 for Yoma; Exodus 12 for Pesahim).

I wish now to dwell on these facts. Formally, redactionally, and linguistically the Mishnah stands in splendid isolation from Scripture. It is not possible to point to many parallels, that is, cases of anonymous books, received as holy, in which the forms and formulations (specific verses) of Scripture play so slight a role. People who wrote holy books commonly imitated the Scripture's language. They cited concrete verses. They claimed at the very least that direct revelation had come to them, as in the angelic discourses of IV Ezra and Baruch, so that what they say stands on an equal plane with Scripture. The internal evidence of the Mishnah's sixty-two usable tractates (excluding Abot), by contrast, in no way suggests that anyone pretended to talk like Moses and write like Moses, claimed to cite and correctly interpret things that Moses had said, or even alleged to have had a revelation like that of Moses and so to stand on the mountain with Moses. There is none of this. So the claim of Scriptural authority for the Mishnah's doctrines and institutions is difficult to locate within the internal evidence of the Mishnah itself.

Let me rapidly survey the conceptual relationships between various Mishnah tractates, on the one side, and laws of Scripture, on the other.

First, there are tractates that simply repeat in their own words precisely what Scripture has to say, and at best serve to amplify and complete the basic ideas of Scripture. For example, all of the cultic tractates of the second division, the one on Appointed Times, which tell what one is supposed to do in the Temple on the various special days of the year, and the bulk of the cultic tractates of the fifth division, which deals with Holy Things, simply restate facts of Scripture. For another example, all of those tractates of the sixth division, on Purities, which specify sources of uncleanness, depend completely on information supplied by Scripture. I have demonstrated in detail that every important statement in Niddah, on menstrual uncleanness, and the most fundamental notions of Zabim, on the uncleanness of the person with flux referred to in Leviticus Chapter Fifteen, as well as every detail in Negaim, on the uncleanness of the person or house suffering the uncleanness described at Leviticus Chapters Thirteen and Fourteen—all of these tractates serve only to reiterate the basic facts of Scripture and to complement those facts with other important ones.

There are, second, tractates which take up facts of Scripture but work them out in a way in which those Scriptural facts cannot have led us to predict. A supposition concerning what is important *about* the facts, utterly remote from the supposition of Scripture, will explain why the Mishnah tractates under discussion say the original things they say in confronting those Scripturally provided facts. For one example, Scripture takes for granted that the red cow will be burned in a state of uncleanness, because it is burned outside the camp—Temple. The priestly writers cannot have imagined that a state of cultic cleanness was to be attained outside of the cult. The absolute datum of tractate Parah, by contrast, is that cultic cleanness not only can be attained outside of the 'tent of meeting.' The red cow was to be burned in a state of cleanness even exceeding that cultic cleanness required in the Temple itself. The problematic that generates the intellectual agendum of Parah, therefore, is how to work out the conduct of the rite of burning the cow in relationship to the Temple: Is it to be done in exactly the same way, or in exactly the opposite way? This mode of contrastive and analogical thinking helps us to understand the generative problematic of such tractates as Erubin and Besah, to mention only two.

Third, there are, predictably, many tractates that either take up problems in no way suggested by Scripture, or begin from facts at best merely relevant to facts of Scripture. In the former category are Tohorot, on the cleanness of foods, with its companion, Uqsin; Demai, on doubtfully tithed produce; Tamid, on the conduct of the daily whole-offering; Baba Batra, on rules of real estate transactions and certain other commercial and property relationships, and so on. In the last category are Ohalot, which spins out its strange problems within the theory that a tent and a utensil are to be compared to one another (!); Kelim, on the susceptibility to uncleanness of various sorts of utensils; Miqvaot, on the sorts of water that effect purification from uncleanness; Ketubot and Gittin, on the documents of marriage and divorce; and many others. These tractates draw on facts of Scripture. But the problem confronted in these tractates in no way responds to problems important to Scripture. What we have here is a prior program of inquiry, which will make ample provision for facts of Scripture in an inquiry generated essentially outside of the framework of Scripture. First comes the problem or topic, then —if possible— comes attention to Scripture.

So there we have it: some tractates merely repeat what we find in Scripture. Some are totally independent of Scripture. And some fall in between. We find everything and its opposite. But to offer a final answer to the question of Scripture-Mishnah relationships, we have to take that fact seriously. The Mishnah in no way is so remote from Scripture as its formal omission of citations of verses of Scripture suggests. It cannot be described as contingent upon, and secondary to Scripture, as many of its third-century apologists claimed. But the right answer is not that it is somewhere in between. Scripture confronts the framers of the Mishnah as revelation, not merely as a source of facts. The framers of the Mishnah had their own world with which to deal. They made statements in the framework and fellowship of their own age and generation. They were bound, therefore, to come to Scripture with a set of questions generated other than in Scripture. They brought their own ideas about what was going to be important in Scripture. This is perfectly natural.

The philosophers of the Mishnah conceded to Scripture the highest authority. At the same time what they chose to hear, within the authoritative statements of Scripture, will in the end form a statement of its own. To state matters simply: all of Scripture is authoritative. But only some of Scripture is relevant. And what happened is that the framers and philosophers of the tradition of the Mishnah came to Scripture when they had reason to. That is to say, they brought to Scripture a program of questions and inquiries framed essentially among themselves. So they were highly selective. That is why their program itself constituted a statement *upon* the meaning of Scripture. They, and their apologists of one sort, hastened to add, that their program consisted of a statement *of*, and upon, the meaning of Scripture.

In part we must affirm the truth of that claim. When the framers of the Mishnah speak about the priestly passages of the Mosaic law codes, with deep insight they perceive profound layers of meaning embedded to begin with in those codes. What they have done with the Priestly Code (P), moreover, they also have done, though I think less coherently, with the bulk of the Deuteronomic laws and with some of those of the Covenant Code. But their exegetical triumph—exegetical, not merely eisegetical—lies in their handling of the complex corpus of materials of the Priestly Code.

The way in which the sages of the Mishnah utilize the inherited and authoritative tradition of Scripture therefore is clear. On the one hand, wherever they can they repeat what Scripture says. This they do, however, in their own words. So they establish a claim of relevance and also authority. They speak to their own day in their own idiom.

On the other hand, they select with care and precision what they want in Scripture, ignoring what they do not want. They take up laws, not prophecies, descriptions of how things are supposed to be, not accounts of what is going to happen. Within the laws they focus upon those pertinent to the cult.

The program of repeating what was familiar provides reassurance. What will be is what was. At the same time saying the obvious contains a polemic and an apologetic. The polemic consists in the implication that the obvious requires restatement. People thus have lost access to the things they should know, to the rules they should keep. Which people? The priests. And who restores the ancient ways? The sages. The apologetic of course flows from the polemic. The Temple was destroyed because of sin. When it is rebuilt, it will follow the laws to which it should have conformed to begin with. The next stage in the argument—not reached in articulated form—can only be this: had the Temple conformed to the law we now state, it would not have been destroyed. So we see the strange spectacle of sages, not priests, presuming to tell priests what to do and how to do it. In this drama we find a partisan account of what has happened, together with a powerful appeal for support to regain the old and stable world of Temple, cult, and celebration, through right knowledge and right action—which only sages can teach.

In their approach to Scripture, the sages of the Mishnah confront the issues of the age with a message of stabilization through restoration. At the same time, they also turn out to settle scores with the priesthood. And, further, they offer a partial answer to the prevailing mood of guilt and despair by at the same time honoring the priesthood and turning it into a scapegoat.

iii. Stability and Syntax

The rigid and disciplined linguistic forms of the Mishnah present, in the mental world of language, a world of order and stability without replication or counterpart in the social world of chaos and disorder.

In ignoring the syntax and morphology of biblical Hebrew in favor of a new language of Hebrew, one essentially their own (in that the Mishnah is the first full picture we have of Mishnaic Hebrew) and authoritative from their time to ours, the framers of the Mishnah engage in a stunningly daring and creative act. They revise the very foundations of mind and intellect, starting fresh. So they say old things in a wholly renewed language, while describing an archaic world in a spirit I have called reactionary. But they do so in ways so fresh and unprecedented as to have defied prediction before their day. I have emphasized that the appeal to Scripture commonplace in Israelite culture—citation, pseudepigraphy, revelation, imitation—is ignored in the Mishnah. The entire repertoire is set aside. The conventions of dealing with the authoritative heritage of Sinai and its revelation are laid by the way. Now we come to the counterpart of this theologico-cultural choice, the new initiative in speech.

The speech patterns exhibited in the Mishnah follow a handful of patterns, all of them rigid and stable. There is, first of all, no room for individual choices of syntax. Everyone expresses whatever he wants to say in the same way as everyone else, within the tiny repertoire of possibilities, which I shall list. Second, the document unfolds in a predictable way, within a logical order and pattern of topics. Indeed, the logic is so self-evident that through an outline of the way in which a topic or theme is unpacked, we may point immediately to the generative problematic accounting for the way in which the topic is unpacked. I mean, the framers of the document do not provide random information. They generally, though not always, frame essays on problems pertinent to a given topic. If you want to know *how* they know what they want to know about that topic, you seek what I call the generative problematic. By this I mean the source of questions about the topic. And, as I have just said, to find that out, you need merely outline their treatment of the topic. That seems to me stunning evidence for their sense of the inner and stable, recoverable, structure of reality. In their hands language is an instrument for the stabilization of the mind, for the disciplining of the chaos of thought. For if you may say things in some few ways, ultimately you also think only some few things. It is typical of intellectuals to imagine that the world is the way you think about it. That, after all, had long been a proposition entertained by the ancient philosophers. How you say what you think, then, becomes a kind of magical formula, as if through the mere saying of things the right way you make a difference. Accordingly, we have now to ask how the sages of the Mishnah expressed their notion of the stability and order of the world through the way in which they expressed their ideas.

Let us start our study of the language of the Mishnah with the simple question of how the document is organized. The answer is that the preferred mode of layout is through themes, spelled out along the lines of the logic embedded in those themes. The Mishnah is divided up—as we already know—into six principal divisions, each expounding a single, immense topic. The tractates of each division take up subtopics of the principal theme. The chapters then unfold along the lines of the (to the framers) logic of the necessary dissection of the division. While that mode of organization may appear to be necessary or "self-evident" (it is how we should have written a law code, is it not?), we should notice that there are three others found within the document, but they are not utilized extensively or systematically. These therefore represent rejected options. One way is to collect diverse sayings around the name of a given authority. (The whole of tractate Eduyot is organized in that way.) A second way is to express a given basic principle through diverse topics, for example, a fundamental rule cutting across many areas of law, stated in one place through all of the diverse types of law through which the rule or principle may be expressed. A third way is to take a striking language pattern and collect sayings on diverse topics which conform to the given language pattern. (There also is the possibility of joining the second and the third ways.) But, faced with these possible ways of organizing materials, the framers of the Mishnah chose to adhere to a highly disciplined thematic-logical principle of organization.

In antiquity paragraphing and punctuation were not commonly used. Long columns of words would contain a text—as in the Torah today—and the student of the text had the task of breaking up those columns into tractates, chapters, sentences, large and small sense units. Now if we had the entire Mishnah in a single immense scroll and spread the scroll out on the ground—perhaps the length of a football field!—we should have no difficulty at all discovering the point, on the five-yard line, at which the first tractate ends and the second begins, and so on down the field to the opposite goal. For from Berakhot at the beginning to Uqsin at the end, the breaking points practically jump up from the ground like white lines of lime: change of principal topic. So the criterion of division, internal to the document and not merely imposed by copyists and printers, is thematic. That is, the tractates are readily distinguishable from one another since each treats a distinct topic. So if, as I said, Mishnah were to be copied out in a long scroll without the significance of lines of demarcation among the several tractates, the opening pericope of each tractate would leave no doubt that one topic had been completed and a new one undertaken.

The same is so within the sixty-two tractates. Intermediate divisions of these same principal divisions are to be discerned on the basis of internal evidence, through the confluence of theme and form. That is to say, a given intermediate division of a principal one (a chapter of a tractate) will be marked by a particular, recurrent, formal pattern in accord with which sentences are constructed, and also by a particular and distinct theme, to which these sentences are addressed. When a new theme commences, a fresh formal pattern will be used. Within the intermediate divisions, we are able to recognize the components, or smallest whole units of thought (hereinafter, cognitive units), because there will be a recurrent pattern of sentence structure repeated time and again within the unit and a shifting at the commencement of the next theme. Each point at which the recurrent pattern commences marks the beginning of a new cognitive unit. In general, an intermediate division will contain a carefully enumerated sequence of exempla of cognitive units, in the established formal pattern, commonly in groups of three or five or multiples of three or five (pairs for the first division).

The cognitive units resort to a remarkably limited repertoire of formulary patterns. Mishnah manages to say whatever it wants in one of the following:

1. The simple declarative sentence, in which the subject, verb, and predicate are tightly joined syntactically to one another, as in *He who does so and so is such and such*

2. The duplicated subject, in which the subject of the sentence is stated twice, as in *He who does so and so, lo, he is such and such*

3. Mild apocopation, in which the subject of the sentence is cut off from the verb, which refers to its own subject, and not the one with which the sentence begins, as in *He who does so and so . . ., it [the thing he has done] is such and such*

4. Extreme apocopation, in which a series of clauses is presented, none of them tightly joined to what precedes or follows, and all of them cut off from the predicate of the sentence, as in *He who does so and so . . ., it [the thing he has done] is such and such . . ., it is a matter of doubt whether . . . or whether . . . lo, it [referring to nothing in the antecedent, apocopated clauses of the subject of the sentence] is so and so . . .*

5. In addition to these formulary patterns, in which the distinctive formulary traits are effected

through variations in the relationship between the subject and the predicate of the sentence, or in which the subject itself is given a distinctive development, there is yet a fifth. In this last one we have a contrastive complex predicate; here we may have two sentences independent of one another yet clearly formulated so as to stand in acute balance with one another in the predicate, as in *He who does . . . is unclean, and he who does not . . . is clean.*

It naturally will be objected: Is it possible that a simple declarative sentence may be asked to serve as a formulary pattern, alongside the rather distinctive and unusual constructions I have listed? True, by itself a tightly constructed sentence consisting of subject, verb, and complement, in which the verb refers to the subject, and the complement to the verb, hardly exhibits traits of particular formal interest. Yet a sequence of such sentences, built along the same gross grammatical lines, may well exhibit a clear-cut and distinctive pattern. When we see that three or five "simple declarative sentences" take up one principle or problem, and then, when the principle or problem shifts, a quite distinctive formal pattern will be utilized, we realize that the "simple declarative sentence" has served the formulator of the unit of thought as aptly as did apocopation, a dispute, or another more obviously distinctive form or formal pattern. The contrastive predicate is one example: the Mishnah contains many more.

The important point of differentiation, particularly for the simple declarative sentence, appears therefore in the intermediate unit, as I just said, thus in the interplay between theme and form. It is there that we see a single pattern recurring in a long sequence of sentences, such as *The X which has lost its Y is unclean because of its Z. The Z which has lost its Y is unclean because of its X.* Another example will be a long sequence of highly developed sentences, laden with relative clauses and other explanatory matter, in which a single syntactical pattern will govern the articulation of three or six or nine exempla. That sequence will be followed by one repeated terse sentence pattern, as *X is so and so, Y is such and such, Z is thus and so.* The former group will treat one principle or theme, the latter some other. There can be no doubt, therefore, that the declarative sentence in recurrent patterns is, in its way, just as carefully formalized as a sequence of severely apocopated sentences or of contrastive predicates or duplicated subjects.

This brief survey of the literary traits of the Mishnah permits us to turn to the question: What is to be learned about the authorities who bear responsibility for the peculiar way in which the Mishnah is formulated and redacted from the way in which they express their ideas? We speak, in particular, of the final generation represented in the Mishnah itself, the authorities of the period ca. A.D. 200, who gave the document its present literary character.

The dominant stylistic trait of the Mishnah as they formulated it is the acute formalization of its syntactical structure and its carefully framed sequences of formalized language, specifically, its intermediate divisions, so organized that the limits of a theme correspond to those of a formulary pattern. The balance and order of the Mishnah are particular to the Mishnah. It now must be asked to testify to the intentions of the people who so made it. Whom does it speak of? And why, in particular, have its authorities distinctively shaped language in rhymes and balanced, matched, declarative sentences, imposing upon the conceptual, factual prose of the law a peculiar kind of poetry? Why do they create rhythmic order, grammatically balanced sentences containing discrete law, laid out in what seem to be carefully enumerated sequences, and the like? Language not only contains culture, which could not exist without it. Language, in our case linguistic and syntactical style and stylization, expresses a world view and ethos. Whose world view is contained and expressed in the Mishnah's formalized rhetoric?

There is no reason to doubt that if one asked the authorities behind the Mishnah the immediate purpose of their systematic use of formalized language, their answer would be to facilitate memorization. For that is the proximate effect of the acute formalization of their document. Much in its character can be seen as mnemonic.

So the Mishnah's is language for an occasion. The occasion is particular: formation and transmission of special sorts of conceptions in a special way. The predominant, referential function of language, giving verbal structure to the message itself, is secondary in our document. The expressive function, conveying the speaker's attitude toward what he is talking about, the conative function, focusing upon who is being addressed, and other ritualized functions of language come to the fore. The Mishnah's language, therefore, as I said, is special, meant as an expression of a nonreferential function. So far as the Mishnah was meant to be memorized by a distinctive group of people for an extraordinary purpose, it is language that includes few and excludes many, unites those who use it and sets them apart from others who do not.

The formal aspects of Mishnaic rhetoric are empty of content. This is proved by the fact that pretty much all themes and conceptions can be reduced to the same few formal patterns. These patterns are established by syntactical recurrences, as distinct from recurrence of sounds. The same words do not recur. Long sequences of patterned and disciplined sentences fail to repeat the same words—that is, syllabic balance, rhythm, or sound—yet they do establish a powerful claim to order and formulary sophistication and perfection. That is why we could name a pattern, *he who . . . it is . . .*—apocopation: the arrangement of the words as a grammatical pattern, not their substance, is indicative of pattern. Accordingly, while we have a document composed along what clearly are mnemonic lines, the Mishnah's susceptibility to memorization rests principally upon the utter abstraction of recurrent syntactical patterns, rather than on the concrete repetition of particular words, rhythms, syllabic counts, or sounds.

A sense of the deep, inner logic of word patterns, of grammar and syntax, rather than of their external similarities, governs the Mishnaic mnemonic. And that yields the fundamental point of this analysis:

even though the Mishnah is to be memorized and handed on orally, it expresses a mode of thought attuned to abstract relationships, rather than concrete and substantive forms. The formulaic, not the formal, character of the Mishnaic rhetoric yields a picture of a subculture—the sages who made up the book—which speaks of immaterial, and not material, things. In this subculture the *relationship*, rather than the thing or person which is related, is primary. The way things come together constitutes the principle of reality. The thing in itself is less than the thing in cathexis with other things, so too the person: you are what you do—in social context. It is self-evident that the repetition of form creates form. But what is repeated, as I have explained, is not external or superficial form. Rather we find formulary patterns of deep syntax, patterns effected through persistent grammatical or syntactical relationships and affecting an infinite range of diverse objects and topics. Form and structure emerge not from concrete, formal things but from abstract and unstated, but ubiquitous and powerful, relationships.

This fact—the creation of pattern through grammatical relationship of syntactical elements, more than through concrete sounds—tells us that the people who memorized conceptions reduced to these particular forms were capable of extraordinarily abstract cognition and perception. Hearing peculiarities of word order in diverse cognitive contexts, their ears and minds perceived regularities of grammatical arrangement. They could catch repeated functional variations of utilization of diverse words. They grasped from such subtleties syntactical patterns not expressed by recurrent external phenomena, such as sounds, rhythms, or key words, and independent of particular meanings. What they heard, it is clear, were not only abstract relationships among parts of speech. They could bring to the surface principles conveyed along with and through these relationships. For, I repeat, what was memorized was a recurrent and fundamental notion, expressed in diverse *examples* but in recurrent rhetorical-syntactical *patterns.* Accordingly, what the memorizing student of a sage could and did hear was what lay far beneath the surface of the rule: the unstated principle within the unsounded pattern of contrast or repetition. This means that the prevalent mode of thought was attuned to what lay beneath the surface; minds and ears perceived what was not said behind what was said and how it was said. They sought that ineffable and metaphysical reality concealed within but conveyed through spoken and palpable material reality.

Social interrelationships within the community of Israel are left behind in the ritual speech of the Mishnah, just as, within the laws, natural realities are made to give form and expression to supernatural or metaphysical regularities. The Mishnah speaks of Israel, but the speakers are a group apart. The Mishnah talks of this-worldly things, but the things stand for and speak of another world entirely—a destroyed Temple in a forbidden city. The language of the Mishnah and its formalized grammatical rhetoric create a world of discourse quite separate from the concrete realities of a given time, place, or society.

The exceedingly limited repertoire of grammatical patterns by which all things on all matters are said gives symbolic expression to the notion that beneath the accidents of life are a few comprehensive relationships. Unchanging and enduring patterns lie deep in the inner structure of reality and impose structure upon the accidents of the world. This means, as I have implied, that reality for Mishnaic rhetoric consists in the grammar and syntax of language: consistent and enduring patterns of relationship among diverse and changing concrete things or persons. What lasts is not the concrete thing but the abstract interplay governing any and all sorts of concrete things.

There is, therefore, a congruence between rhetorical patterns of speech, on the one side, and the substantive framework of discourse established by these same patterns, on the other. Just as we accomplish memorization by perceiving not what is said but how it is said and is persistently arranged, so we speak to undertake to address and describe a world in which what is concrete and material is secondary. How things are said about what is concrete and material in diverse ways and contexts is principal. The Mishnah is silent about the context of its speech—place and time and circumstance—because context is trivial: from no one in particular to whom it may concern. Principle, beginning in syntactical principles by which all words are arranged in a severely limited repertoire of grammatical sentences ubiquitously pertinent but rarely made explicit, is at the center.

The skill of the formulators of the Mishnah is to

manipulate the raw materials of everyday speech. What they have done is to structure language so as to make it strange, to impose a fresh perception upon what to others are merely unpatterned and ordinary ways of saying things. *What* is said in the Mishnah is simple. *How* it is said is arcane. Ordinary folk cannot have had much difficulty understanding the words, which refer to routine actions and objects. How long it must have taken to grasp the meaning of the patterns into which the words are arranged! How hard it was and is to do so is suggested (at the very least) by the necessity for the creation of Tosefta (supplements), the Talmuds (commentaries to the Mishnah), and the commentaries in the long centuries since the Mishnah came into being. In this sense the Mishnah speaks openly about public matters, yet its deep structure of syntax and grammatical forms shapes what is said into an essentially secret and private language. It takes many years to master the difficult argot, though only a few minutes to memorize the simple patterns. That constitutes a paradox reflective of the situation of the creators of the Mishnah.

Up to now I have said only a little about tense structure. The reason is that the Mishnah exhibits remarkable indifference to the potentialities of meaning inherent therein. Its persistent preference for the plural participle—thus the descriptive present tense—"they do . . .," "one does . . ."—is matched by its capacity to accept the mixture of past, present, and future tenses. These can be found jumbled together in a single sentence and, even more commonly, in a single pericope. It follows that the Mishnah is remarkably uninterested in differentiation of time sequences. This fact is most clearly shown by the *gemisch* of the extreme-apocopated sentence with its capacity to support something like the following: "He who does so and so . . . the rain came and wet it down . . . if he was happy . . . it [is] under the law, if water be put." Clearly, the matter of tense, past, present, future, is conventional. Highly patterned syntax clearly is meant to preserve what is said without change (even though we know changes in the wording of traditions were effected for many centuries thereafter). The language is meant to be unshakeable. Its strict rules of rhetoric are meant not only to convey, but also to preserve, equally strict rules of logic, equally permanent patterns of relationship. What was at stake in this formation of language in the service of permanence? Clearly, how things were said was intended to secure eternal preservation of what was said. Change affects the accidents and details. It cannot reshape enduring principles. Language will be used to effect and protect their endurance. What is said, moreover, is not to be subjected to pragmatic experimentation. Unstated but carefully considered principles shape reality. They are not shaped and tested by and against reality. Use of pat phrases and syntactical clichés, divorced from different thoughts to be said and different ways of thinking, testifies to the prevailing notion of unstated, but secure and unchanging, reality behind and beneath the accidents of context and circumstance: God is one, God's world is in order, each line carefully drawn, all structures fully coherent.

So there are these two striking traits of mind reflected within Mishnaic rhetoric; first, the perception of order and balance; second, the perception of the mind's centrality in the construction of order and balance, that is, the imposition of wholeness upon discrete cases in the case of the routine declarative sentence and upon discrete phrases in the case of the apocopated one. Both order and balance are contained from within and are imposed from without. The relationships revealed by grammatical consistencies internal to a sentence and the implicit regularities revealed by the congruence and cogency of cases rarely are stated. But they always are to be discerned. Accordingly, the one thing which Mishnah invariably does not make explicit but which always is necessary to know is, I stress, the presence of the active intellect, the participant who is the hearer. It is the hearer who ultimately makes sense of, perceives the sense in, the Mishnah. Once more we are impressed by the Mishnah's expectation of high sophistication and profound sensitivity to order and form in its impalpable audience. Again we note that, to the Mishnah, the human mind imposes meaning and sense upon the world of sense perceptions.

To conclude this discussion, we turn to Wittgenstein's saying "The limits of my language mean the limits of my world." On the one side, the Mishnah's formulaic rhetoric imposes limits, boundaries, upon the world. What fits into that rhetoric and can be said by it constitutes world, world given shape and boundary by the Mishnah. The Mishnah implicitly maintains, therefore, that a wide range of things falls within the territory mapped out by a limited number of linguistic conventions, grammatical sentences. What is grammatical can be said and, therefore, constitutes part of the reality created by the Mishnaic word. What cannot be contained within the grammar of the sentence cannot be said and therefore falls outside the realm of the Mishnaic reality. The Mishnaic reality consists in those things that can attain order, balance, and principle. Chaos lies without.

On the other side, if we may extrapolate from the capacity of the impoverished repertoire of grammar before us to serve for *all* sorts of things, then we must concede that all things can be said by formal revision. Everything can be reformed, reduced to the order and balance and exquisite sense for the just match, characteristic of the Mishnaic pericope. Anything of which we wish to speak is susceptible to the ordering and patterning of the Mishnaic grammar and syntax. That is a fact implicit throughout the Mishnah. Accordingly, the territory mapped out by the Mishnaic language encompasses the whole of the pertinent world under discussion. There are no thematic limitations of the Mishnaic formalized speech.

Clearly, the Mishnah is formulated in a disciplined and systematic way. We therefore must now ask how the language of the Mishnah adumbrates the character and concerns of the Mishnah's substantive ideas, its religious world view and the way of life formulated to express that world view. For I maintain that the document before us constitutes much more than an ancient rulebook, of no special interest or humanistic value, which happens to have survived. The

Mishnah is, rather, a book deliberately formed for the very group, Israel, and purpose which, for nearly nineteen centuries, it indeed has served. So the language just now described, as much as the system awaiting description, has to be asked to testify to the meaning and purpose of the whole.

The "Judaism" expressed by the Mishnah not only speaks about values. Its mode of speech—the way it speaks, not only what it says—is testimony to its highest and most enduring, distinctive value. Now let us take note. This language does not speak of sacred symbols but of pots and pans, of menstruation and dead creeping things, of ordinary water which, because of the circumstance of its collection and location, possesses extraordinary power; of the commonplace corpse and ubiquitous diseased person; of genitalia and excrement, toilet seats and the flux of penises, of stems of pomegranates and stalks of leeks; of rain and earth and wood, metal, glass and hide. This language is filled with words for neutral things of humble existence. It does not speak of holy things and is not symbolic in its substance. This language speaks of ordinary things, of things everyone must have known. But because of the peculiar and particular way in which it is formed and formalized, this same language not only adheres to an aesthetic theory but expresses a deeply embedded ontology and methodology of the sacred, specifically of the sacred within the secular, and of the capacity for regulation, therefore for sanctification, within the ordinary: all things in order, all things, then, hallowed by God who orders all things, so said the priests' creation-tale.

iv. From Sources and Style to Substance

We now know three things: the context in which the Mishnah came into being, the way in which the creators of the Mishnah utilized the antecedent heritage of their people and community, and the traits of language through which they expressed their ideas. These define the document in every way but the important one. They tell us nothing about its principal message, what it has to say to its day, its message drawn from the antecedent tradition, what it proposes to express through its mode of saying what it wants. We know that the Mishnah's framers had the elemental problem of finding something to say when history had left nothing worth saying. We now realize that they made ample use of the facts and ideas of Scripture, so founding their claim to be obeyed upon the authority of Scripture. We recognize that they made up a language which, in its external traits of form, in its manipulation of the deep structures of syntax, would prove congruent to their intellects as scholars and philosophers. All that we now lack is a clear picture of what they wished to tell people about themselves, that is, about Israel beyond catastrophe. And, in the nature of things, we have now to describe a world view embodied in a way of life—a Judaism (in this context). Our task is now to come to the point.

CHAPTER THREE

Sanctification in an Age of Pollution

i. The Temple at the Center

When the general and messiah Bar Kokhba issued coins, he imprinted on them "The Freedom of Israel. Year One" and "The Freedom of Israel. Year Two." (There are not many in the sequence for Year Three.) In Bar Kokhba's formulation, the word "freedom" carried the weight of the hope of Israel. Accordingly, the crisis of the aftermath of the two lost wars should have been formulated in terms of freedom and slavery, victory and defeat, hope and despair—in all, in the categories of history, apocalypse, and prophecy. Had it been produced within the framework of Bar Kokhba's formulation of the critical issues confronting Israel, the Jewish people, the Mishnah would surely have taken up other topics, of greater importance, than the topics it treats: the meaning of politics and history, not the planting of seeds and the formation of families and society. In describing the religious world view of the sages of the Mishnah, seeing the Temple at the center, I of course replicate their viewpoint. But the Mishnah's program, issues, perspectives on what is important to the life and destiny of Israel, the Jewish people—these do not define the sole possibility. There were (as there are today) alternatives. In placing the destruction of the Temple at the center of the crisis of the later first and second centuries in the history of Judaism, we find ourselves repeating, rather than analyzing, the viewpoint of the sources subject to our analysis.

From the viewpoint of those sources, based as they are on the thousand-year-old tradition of the priesthood, the Temple stood for life against death. The reason was that there the transfer of sustenance took place from earth to heaven. The Book of Leviticus left no doubt about that fact. Rules of careful antisepsis permitted the God to come; the sacrifices were God's meals. These ideas were commonplace in the explanation of temples and cults in general and took shape merely within the Israelite idiom, both in the ancient Scriptures and in the later writings of priests and their followers. The priests, for their part, ate part of the meals prepared for God. They ate in accord with the same rules by which God's meals were made ready and protected. The way priests ate their food in the Temple, that is, the cultic rules and conditions observed in that setting, was like the way God ate his food in the Temple. That is to say, God's food and locus of nourishment were to be protected from the same sources of danger and contamination, preserved in the same exalted condition of sanctification. So by acting, that is, eating, like God, Israel became like God: a pure and perfect incarnation, on earth in the land which was holy, of the model of heaven. Eating food was the critical act and occasion, just as the priestly authors of Leviticus and Numbers had maintained when they made laws governing slaughtering beasts and burning up their flesh, baking pancakes and cookies with and without olive oil and burning them on the altar. The nourishment of the land—meat, grain, oil, and wine—was set before God and burned ("offered up") in conditions of perfect cultic antisepsis.

In context this antisepsis provided protection against things deemed the opposite of nourishment, the quintessence of death: corpse matter, people who looked like corpses (Lev. 13), dead creeping things, blood when not flowing in the veins of the living, such as menstrual blood (Lev. 15), and other sorts of flux (semen in men, nonmenstrual blood in women) that yield not life but then its opposite, so death. What these excrescences have in common, of course, is that they are ambivalent. Why? Because they may be one thing or the other. Blood in the living is the soul: blood not in the living is the soul of contamination. The corpse was once a living person, like God: the person with skin like a corpse's who looks dead was once a person who looked alive: the flux of the *zab* (Lev. 15) comes from the flaccid penis, which under the right circumstances, that is, properly erect, produces semen and makes life. What is at the margin between life and death and can go either way is what is the source of uncleanness. But, as I shall stress, that is insufficient. For in the Priestly Code the opposite of *unclean* is not only *clean*, but also *holy*. The antonym is not to be missed: death or life, unclean or holy.

Bar Kokhba would not have framed the issues of life and death in this way. True, vast numbers of Jews gave their lives on the battlefield in his cause. But what they died for, as I said, was freedom from foreign rule of the Holy Land, the right to make their own decisions for their nation, including, of course, the right to rebuild the Temple and reinstitute the sacrificial cult. If all that was at issue was life represented by cultic cleanness as against death embodied in pollution, why take up arms when all you had to do was take a bath? In phrasing matters in this gross way, of course, I draw a sharp contrast between one faction and another of what was, in the end, a single community sharing a common corpus of convictions. We know, for example, that Bar Kokhba was as observant as any other Jew of his day. We need not doubt priests and some scribes and sages too fought in his ranks. And yet there are a disproportion and a discontinuity. In the cosmic drama embodied in the Temple's rites and sacrifices, there was no place for the sword, only a slaughter knife, the hero was not a soldier but a priest, a kind of holy butcher. The Mishnah is a book about the cult, though it contains a few rules on making war. If Bar Kokhba's scribes had written a book of this kind, I suspect it would be more like the Dead Sea scroll containing the rules for the War of the Sons of Light against the Sons of Darkness than it would resemble the Mishnah. True, there would be rules for the cult. But the law code of holy wars would not be about the cult, any more than the Mishnah, with its curious amalgam of scribal mentality and priestly obsession, is about fighting battles in this world and against the Romans.

So for the Mishnah the cult is the point of struggle between the forces of life and nourishment and the forces of death and extinction: meat, grain, oil, and wine, against corpse matter, dead creeping things, blood in the wrong setting, semen in the wrong context, and the like. Then, on the occasions when meat was eaten, mainly at the time of festivals or other moments at which sin offerings and peace offerings were made, people who wished to live ate their meat, and at all times ate the staples of wine, oil, and bread, in a state of life—that is, cultic cleanness—and so generated life. They kept their food and themselves away from the state of death, cultic uncleanness, as much as possible. And this heightened reality pertained at home, as much as in the Temple, where most rarely went on ordinary days. The Temple was the font of life, the bulwark against death.

ii. The Mishnah's System of Sanctification

The Mishnah, for its part, takes up the fundamental perspectives of the Priestly Code, with stress on the twin opposites of sanctification and pollution. But it forms a system of its own, related to but separate from, that of the Priestly Code. Accordingly, we should take a moment to review in its own terms the large-scale design of the Mishnah.

The Judaism shaped by the Mishnah consists of a

coherent world view and comprehensive way of living. It is a world view that speaks of transcendent things, a way of life in response to the supernatural meaning of what is done, a heightened and deepened perception of the sanctification of Israel in deed and in deliberation. Sanctification means two things: first, distinguishing Israel in all its dimensions from the world in all its ways; second, establishing the stability, order, regularity, predictability, and reliability of Israel at moments and in contexts of danger. Danger means instability, disorder, irregularity, uncertainty, and betrayal. Each topic of the system as a whole takes up a critical and indispensable moment or context of social being. Each orders what is disorderly and dangerous. Through what is said in regard to each of the Mishnah's principal topics, what the system as a whole wishes to declare is fully expressed. Yet if the parts severally and jointly give the message of the whole, the whole cannot exist without all of the parts, so well-joined and carefully crafted are they all.

Let me now describe and briefly interpret the six components of the Mishnah's system. The critical issue in the economic life, which means in farming, is in two parts, revealed in the first division. First, Israel, as tenant on God's holy land, maintains the property in the ways God requires, keeping the rules that mark the land and its crops as holy. Next, the hour at which the sanctification of the land comes to form a critical mass, namely, in the ripened crops, is the moment ponderous with danger and heightened holiness. Israel's will so affects the crops as to mark a part of them as holy, the rest of them as available for common use. The human will is determinative in the process of sanctification.

In the second division, what happens in the land at certain times, at Appointed Times, marks off spaces of the land as holy in yet another way. The center of the land and the focus of its sanctification is the Temple. There the produce of the land is received and given back to God, the one who created and sanctified the land. At these unusual moments of sanctification, the inhabitants of the land in their social being in villages enter a state of spatial sanctification. That is to say, the village boundaries mark off holy space, within which one must remain during the holy time. This is expressed in two ways. First, the Temple itself observes and expresses the special, recurring holy time. Second, the villages of the land are brought into alignment with the Temple, forming a complement and completion to the Temple's sacred being. The advent of the appointed times precipitates a spatial reordering of the land, so that the boundaries of the sacred are matched and mirrored in village and in Temple. At the heightened holiness marked by these moments of Appointed Times, therefore, the occasion for an affective sanctification is worked out. Like the harvest, the advent of an appointed time, a pilgrim festival, also a sacred season, is made to express that regular, orderly, and predictable sort of sanctification for Israel which the system as a whole seeks.

If for a moment we now leap over the next two divisions, the third and fourth, we come to the counterpart of the divisions of Agriculture and Appointed Times. These are the Fifth and Sixth divisions, namely, Holy Things and Purities. They deal with the everyday and the ordinary, as against the special moments of harvest, on the one side, and special time or season, on the other.

The fifth division is about the Temple on ordinary days. The Temple, the locus of sanctification, is conducted in a wholly routine and trustworthy, punctilious manner. The one thing that may unsettle matters is the intention and will of the human actor. This actor, the priest, is subjected to carefully prescribed limitations and remedies. The division of Holy Things generates its companion, the Sixth division, the one on cultic cleanness, Purities. The relationship between the two is like that between Agriculture and Appointed Times, the former locative, the latter utopian, the former dealing with the fields, the latter with the interplay between fields and altar.

Here too, in the sixth division, once we speak of the one place of the Temple, we address, too, the cleanness that pertains to every place. A system of cleanness, taking into account what imparts uncleanness and how this is done, what is subject to uncleanness and how that state is overcome—that system is fully expressed in response to the participation of the human will. Without the wish and act of a human being, the system does not function. It is inert. Sources of uncleanness, which come naturally and not by volition, and modes of purification, which work naturally and not by human intervention, are inert. Only the human will can impart susceptibility to uncleanness. That is, the human being alone can introduce into the system, that food and drink, bed, pot, chair, and pan, which to begin with form the focus of the system. The movement from sanctification to uncleanness takes place when human will and work precipitate it.

This now brings us back to the middle divisions, the third and fourth, on Women and Damages. They take their place in the structure of the whole by showing the congruence, within the larger framework of regularity and order, of human concerns of family and farm, politics and workaday transactions among ordinary people. For without attending to these matters, the Mishnah's system does not encompass what, at its foundations, it is meant to comprehend and order: Israel's whole life. So what is at issue is fully cogent with the rest.

In the case of Women, the third division, attention focuses upon the point of disorder marked by the transfer of that disordering anomaly, woman, from the regular status provided by one man to the equally trustworthy status provided by another. That is the point at which the Mishnah's interests are aroused: once more, predictably, the moment of disorder.

In the case of Damages, the fourth division, there are two important concerns. First, there is the paramount interest in preventing, so far as possible, the disorderly rise of one person and fall of another, and in sustaining the status quo of the economy, the house and household, of Israel, the holy society in eternal stasis. Second, there is the necessary concomitant in the provision of a system of political institutions to carry out the laws that preserve the balance and steady state of persons.

The two divisions that take up topics of concrete and material concern—the formation and dissolution of families and the transfer of property in that connection and the resultant potential dislocation of the state of families in society—are both locative and utopian. They deal with the concrete locations in which people make their lives, household and street and field, the sexual and commercial exchanges of a given village. But they pertain to the life of all Israel, both in the land and otherwise. These two divisions, together with the household ones of Appointed Times, constitute the sole opening outward toward the life of utopian Israel, that diaspora in the far reaches of the ancient world, in the endless span of time. This community, from the Mishnah's perspective, is not only in exile but unaccounted for, outside the system, for the Mishnah declines to recognize and take it into account. Israelites who dwell in the land of (unclean) death instead of in the land simply fall outside of the range of (holy) life. Priests, who must remain cultically clean, may not leave the land—and neither may most of the Mishnah.

So the six components of the Mishnah's system insist upon two things: first, stability; second, order. They define as a problem something somehow out of line, therefore dangerous. Laws for a woman must be made, in particular when she changes hands, moving from father to husband, or, in divorce, husband to father. Laws for the governance of civil transactions must make certain that all transactions produce equal and opposite results. No one must emerge larger than when he entered, none must emerge diminished. Equal value must be exchanged, or a transaction is null. The advent of sacred time, as we shall see, not only imposes the opposite of the Temple's rules upon the village. The holy day also has the effect of linking the Israelite to one place, a particular place, his or her village. So for a moment sacred time establishes a tableau and creates a diorama, a still place of perfection in a silent and perfected moment. Since, as I said, the Mishnah emerges out of the viewpoint of the Priestly Codes of Scripture, we must expect its generative word choices to conform to that of those codes. So the Mishnah will speak, as we know full well, not about disorder and stabilization, but rather about pollution, on the one side, and (beyond purification) sanctification on the other.

iii. Holy and Unclean

In the priestly code of Leviticus, as I said, one principal antonym for holy is unclean. (The other is profane.) In the law of the Mishnah, the Land of Israel *is* holy. Its soil alone is cultically clean. All the other lands are unclean. In the Land of Israel there are, moreover, gradations of holiness, rising, at the pinnacle, to the Temple at the top, the apex of life. The destruction of the Temple (as Ezekiel had said the time before) diminished the holiness that had been in the world before. Pollution in the form of uncleanness of persons and animate beings, listed in Leviticus 11–15, had been removed, in part, through rites in the Temple. With the Temple in ruins and even inaccessible, there was no way to remove not only guilt but uncleanness.

When, therefore, I speak of sanctification in a time of pollution, I do not mean to use these words in any metaphorical sense. To the Israelites of this time, pollution and sanctification were real and concrete. In accord with the biblical laws, there were things you could not do if you were unclean: there also were times of sanctification. As I said, Israel in its land remained the holy people in the holy land. Accordingly, the issue of how to deal with pollution and to effect sanctification was not theological but material and worldly, just as the destruction of the Temple was an event of surpassing consequence in the here and now.

At the same time, if we wish to define in the Mishnah's context the meaning of sanctification and its antonym, we have first of all to ask, a definition for what purpose? That is to say, a definition can be judged adequate only if it serves a stated purpose, which then allows us to know whether the definition indeed is adequate to its purpose. If you asked a Temple priest why someone would want to go from being cultically unclean to being cultically clean, the answer would be, "So as to participate in the Temple and its rites." If, by extension, you were to ask a Pharisee of the first century why he wished to be cultically clean, he would have told you, "So as to eat my ordinary food as if I were eating the food of the priests in the Temple of the Lord." Here too the purpose of being clean, hence the meaning of being unclean, is self-evident: clean for the cult. After 135 why should people have cared if they were unclean, since, when the Temple had stood, the principal consideration of uncleanness and of cleanness pertained, as is clear, to the possibility of entering and participating in the Temple rites? The definition of sanctification is still less clear to me. What people could do when they were cultically clean which they could not do when they were cultically unclean, we know full well. But what they could do if they were sanctified which they were unable to do if they were not—and what they *were* if they were not sanctified—I cannot say.

Since our principal point of interest in the Mishnah is to ask it to tell us how something becomes holy and what the meaning of holiness is, we must ask the Mishnah to provide guidance. Specifically, what is a context in which the Mishnah uses the word "sanctification"? For what purpose does something or someone become sanctified? The answer to that question is easy to find, since the Mishnah contains a tractate dealing with "sanctification." Its problem, specifically, is when a woman becomes betrothed, or "sanctified," to a given man. That fact draws our attention still further to the larger framework of discourse on women and their status. At what point in the life of a woman do the framers of the Mishnah take an interest in her? If we may uncover the answer to that question, we shall have some insight into the further question of why the issue of sanctification is invoked, and what is meant thereby. Women present a key to the system as a whole.

iv. Sanctification and Women

The principal interest for the Mishnah is the point at which a woman becomes, and ceases to be, holy to a particular man, that is, enters and leaves the marital union. These transfers of women are the dangerous and disorderly points in the relationship of woman to man, therefore, as I said, to society as well. There is in the Division of Women a clearly defined and neatly conceived system of laws, not about women in general, but concerning what is important about women to the framers of the Mishnah. This is the transfer of women and related property from one domain, the father's, to another, the husband's, and back. The whole constitutes a significant part of the Mishnah's encompassing system of sanctification, for the reason that Heaven confirms what men do on earth. A correctly prepared writ of divorce on earth changes the status of the woman to whom it is given, so that in Heaven she is available for sanctification to some other man, while, without that same writ, in Heaven's view, should she go to some other man, she would be liable to be put to death. The earthly deed and the Heavenly perspective correlate. That is indeed very much part of a larger system, which says the same thing over and over again.

To the message and the purpose of the system of

Women, woman is essential and central. But she is not critical. She sets the stage for the processes of the sacred. It is she who can be made sacred to man. It is she who ceases to stand within a man's sacred circle. But God and man, the latter through the documentary expression of his will and intention, possess the active power of sanctification. Like the holy land of Agriculture, the holy Temple of Holy Things, and the potentially holy realm of the clean of Purities, women for the Division of Women define a principal part of the Mishnah's orderly conception of reality. Women form a chief component of the six-part realm of the sacred. It is, as I said, their position in the social economy of the Israelite reality, natural and supernatural, which is the subject of the Division and its tractates. But the whole—the six-part realm—is always important in relationship to man on earth and God in Heaven. Man and God effect the transaction. Santification is effected through process and through relationship. The center of tension is at critical relationships. The problematic of the subject is generated at the critical points of the relationship. The relationship—that is, the process of transaction—is what makes holy or marks as profane. God and man shape that process. Food grown from the earth, woman, cult, and the realm of the clean—these foci of the sacred form that inert matter made holy or marked as profane by the will and deed of God and of man, who is like God.

From the Mishnah's perspective, women are abnormal, men are normal. The reason the framers of the Mishnah choose to work out a Division on women flows from that fact. Women are something out of the ordinary. That is why they form a focus of sanctification: restoration of the extraordinary to the ordinary and the normal. The Mishnah cannot declare a dead, creeping thing clean. The Mishnah cannot make women into men. It can provide for the purification of what is made unclean. It can provide for a world in which it is normal for woman to be subject to man, father or husband, and a system which regularizes the transfer of women from the hand of the father to that of the husband. The regulation of the transfer of women is the Mishnah's way of effecting the sanctification of what, for the moment, disturbs and disorders the orderly world. The work of sanctification becomes necessary in particular at the point of danger and disorder. An order of women must be devoted, therefore, to just these things, so as to preserve the normal modes of creation ("how these things really are"). Maleness, that is, normality, thus may encompass all, even and especially at the critical point of transfer.

In this connection the process outlined in the Division of Purities for the restoration of normality, meaning of cleanness, to what is abnormal, meaning uncleanness, is suggestive. What the Mishnah proposes is to restore the equilibrium disturbed by the encounter with the disruptive, disorganizing, and abnormal sources of uncleanness specified in the priestly writings. So the Division of Purities centers attention on the point of abnormality and its restoration to normality: sources of uncleanness, foci of uncleanness, modes of purification. Now, when we reflect on the view of women contained in the Mishnah, we observe a parallel interest in the point of abnormality and restoration to normality of women: the moment at which a woman changes hands.

An anomaly for the Mishnah is a situation requiring human intervention so that affairs may be brought into stasis, that is, made to conform with the Heavenly projections of the created world. That quest for stasis, order, and regulation, which constitute wholeness and completeness, in the Division of Women leads the Mishnah to take up yet another circumstance of uncertainty. This it confronts at its most uncertain: just as the Division of Agriculture treats crops neither holy nor secular, so the system subjects the anomaly of woman to the capacity for ordering and regulating which is the gift and skill of priests and scribes.

The anomaly of woman therefore is addressed at its most anomalous. Yet the very essence of the anomaly, woman's sexuality, is scarcely mentioned. But it always is just beneath the surface. For what defines the woman's status—rarely made explicit in the Division of Women—is not whether or not she may have sexual relations but with whom she may have them and with what consequence. It is assumed that, from long before the advent of puberty, a girl may be married and in any event is a candidate for sexuality. From puberty onward she will be married. But what is selected for intense and continuing concern is with whom she may legitimately marry, and with what economic and social effect. There is no sexual deed without public consequence, and only rarely will a sexual deed not yield economic results, in the transfer of property from one hand to another. So what is anomalous is the woman's sexuality, which is treated in a way wholly different from man's. And the goal and purpose of the Mishnah's Division of Women are to bring under control and force into stasis all of the wild and unruly potentialities of sexuality, with their dreadful threat of uncontrolled shifts in personal status and material possession alike.

The Mishnah thus invokes Heaven's interest in the most critical moment—whether Appointed Times or harvest time or hymeneal season—for individual and society alike. Its conception is that what is rightly done on earth is confirmed in Heaven. A married woman who has sexual relations with any man but her husband has not merely committed a crime on earth. She has sinned against Heaven. It follows that when a married woman receives a writ of divorce and so is free to enter into relationships with any man of her choosing, Heaven's perceptions of that woman are affected just as much as are those of man on earth. What was beforehand a crime and a sin afterward is holy. The woman may contract a new marriage on earth which Heaven, for its part, will oversee and sanctify. What is stated in these simple propositions is that those crucial and critical turnings at which a woman changes hands produce concern and response in Heaven above as much as on earth below. And the reason, as I suggested at the beginning, is that Heaven is invoked specifically at those times, and in those circumstances, in which Mishnah confronts a situation of anomaly, changes, or disorder and proposes to effect suitable regulation and besought order.

v. Sanctification, Time and Space

The Priestly Code lays stress on the Sabbath as the climax of creation and the occasion for sanctification. We are not surprised to find an entire division, with a tractate on the Sabbath at its head, devoted to special, or holy, seasons and times. In our inquiry into the Mishnaic conception of sanctification, we find yet another occasion to inquire into the expression of the conception of sanctification. What we find is striking. When a holy day comes, the village enters into the framework of the Temple—only as its mirror image, as I shall explain. Accordingly, the effect of holy time is to translate the ordinary into the holy, hence the village into a replication of the model of the holy in the Temple. Let me now unpack this puzzling conception.

The Mishnaic Division of Appointed Times forms a system in which the advent of a holy day, like the Sabbath of creation, sanctifies the life of the Israelite village by imposing on the village rules on the model of those of the Temple. The purpose of the system, therefore, is to bring into alignment the moment of sanctification of the village and the life of the home with the moment of sanctification of the Temple on those same occasions of appointed times. The underlying and generative theory of the system is that the village is the mirror image of the Temple. If things are done in one way in the Temple, they will be done in the opposite way in the village. Together the village and the Temple on the occasion of the holy day therefore form a single continuum, a completed creation, thus awaiting sanctification.

The village is made like the Temple in that on appointed times one may not freely cross the lines distinguishing the village from the rest of the world, just as one may not freely cross the lines distinguishing the Temple from the world. But the village is a mirror image of the Temple. The boundary lines prevent free entry into the Temple, so they restrict free egress from the village. On the holy day what one may do in the Temple is precisely what one may not do in the village. So the advent of the holy day affects the village by bringing it into sacred symmetry in such wise as to effect a system of opposites; each is holy in a way precisely the opposite of the other. Because of the underlying conception of perfection attained through the union of opposites, the village is not represented as conforming to the model of the cult, but of constituting its antithesis.

The world thus regains perfection when on the holy day heaven and earth are united, the whole completed and done: the heaven, the earth, and all their hosts. This moment of perfection renders the events of ordinary time, of "history," essentially irrelevant. For what really matters in time is that moment in which sacred time intervenes and effects the perfection formed of the union of heaven and earth, of Temple, in the model of the former, and Israel, its complement. It is not a return to a perfect time but recovery of perfect being, a fulfillment of creation, which explains the essentially ahistorical character of the Mishnah's Division on Appointed Times. Sanctification constitutes an ontological category and is effected by the Creator.

When we remember that the notion of an appointed time bears a quite other meaning than the one I have outlined, we realize that the Mishnah's choice is fresh and surprising. For, throughout the antecedent religious systems of Israel, an appointed time was an occasion on which something would happen: the birth of a child, the coming of the messiah. The fulfillment of time meant a climax of history. So the contrast before us is clear. The Mishnah does not speak of onetime historical events. Rather, the Mishnah refers in Appointed Times solely to recurrent events embedded in the regular lunar calendar, defined, in nature, by the movement of the seasons and the moon, and, in Scripture, in the main by the affairs of the cult. The festivals are important in the cult and its counterpart. What recurs is the perfection of creation through the reunion of opposites. That is what is expressed in the Mishnah's problems and laws.

When the Mishnah speaks of appointed times, it means not the end time, or the onetime fulfillment of time, but recurrent Sabbaths and festivals, new moons and holy days. When the Mishnah asks what is to be done in response to those appointed times of nature and cult, it answers in terms of cooking and eating, working and resting, sleeping, celebrating and rejoicing. The Mishnah's program for Sabbaths and festivals speaks not of a being other than the ordinary life of Israel, but of a heightened enjoyment of everyday pleasures. The reason is not a rejection of cosmic myth but the compelling presence of a different myth of being. The Mishnah does not contemplate some age other than the present one. When it speaks of time, it does not mean history at all. (Indeed, in the Division of Damages, the Mishnah finds it possible to design a complete political system without once referring to historical reality or making provision at any point whatsoever for time and change.) The framers of the document, moreover, so lay out matters that the sole provision in the village is for comfort and relaxation. If there is interest in that realm of power and force in which the mythological cosmic drama is played out, that heightened reality of mythic being realized in the holy time of sabbaths and festivals is not permitted to come to expression at all in the Mishnah's restrictive terms. The reason for the Mishnah's worldliness is its otherworldly conception of the this-worldly life of Israel. What corresponds to heaven and complements heaven is heaven's projection onto earth, the Israelites in their villages. Here we have a different cosmic myth, one that speaks of different things to different people.

If we may link the situation of the framers of the Mishnah to their conception of time, we may simply state that the sages whose ideas are before us have had enough of history to last them for eternity. What the Mishnah really wants is for nothing to happen. The Mishnah presents a tableau, a wax museum, a diorama. It portrays a world fully perfected and so fully at rest. The one thing the Mishnah does not want to tell us is about change, how things come to be what they are. That is why there can be no sustained attention to the priesthood and its rules, the scribal profession and its constitution, the class of householders and its interests. The Mishnah's pretense is that all of these have come to rest. They compose a world in stasis, perfect and complete, made holy because it is complete and perfect. It is an economy—again in the classic sense of the word—awaiting the divine act of sanctification which, as at the creation of the world, would set the seal of holy rest upon an again complete creation, just as in the beginning: "Thus the heaven and the earth were finished, and all the host of them. And on the seventh day God finished his work which he had done, and he rested on the seventh day and hallowed it, because on it God rested from all his work which he had done in creation" (Gen. 2:1-3).

vi. Sanctification and Man: The Centrality of the Will

When we reflect that, in times of upheaval and disaster, Israelite prophets and sages addressed the question of man's destiny and his deeds, we may not be surprised to discover at the center of the Mishnah's theory of sanctification the definitive role of man. If we refer back to the destruction of the first Temple in 586, we find that the prophets, before and afterward, reflected on the question, what can a man do? The object of reflection was to sort out the relationship between what Israel had been told to do and what it actually had done. This reflection was meant to explain what had happened and what had to be done to straighten matters out (to understate things). Israel had been told to obey God's will. If, as the Deuteronomic picture goes, Israel does so, it will prosper, and, if not, it will suffer. Since Israel had suffered, it was clear to the prophets before 586, and still more obvious to those afterward, that Israel had not done God's will.

The issue was whether man could do God's will. That is to say, the relationship of the nature and will of man and the word of God had to be spelled out. Jeremiah's solution to this problem lay in his prophecy of the new covenant, written on the heart. He meant to say, therefore, that, in time to come, it would be natural for man to will and to do what God wants: "I will put my law within them, and I will write it upon their hearts" (Jer. 31:33). We cannot be surprised to find profound reflection upon this same theme in the apocalypse in the name of Ezra, who speaks of the nature of man: "O thou, Adam, what has thou done! For though it was thou that sinned, the fall was not thine alone, but ours also, who are thy descendants! For how does it profit us that the eternal age is promised to us, whereas we have done the works that bring death?" (IV Ezra 7:119–20). Reflecting within the matrix of the whole Israelite heritage, Paul confesses, "I do not understand my own actions. For I do not do what I want, but I do everything I hate. Now if I do what I do not want, I agree that the law is good. So that it is no longer I that do it, but sin which dwells within me. . . . I can will what is right, but I cannot do it. For I do not do the good I want, but the evil I do not want is what I do. Now if I do what I do not want, it is no longer I that do it, but sin which dwells within me" (Romans 7:15–20). In citing these reflections on the nature of sin in relationship to the will and works of man, I mean only to point out one fact. The issue of what happens to Israel is going to be phrased in terms of what Israel does, and what Israel does is measured against what Israel wills. Accordingly, the issue of the will of man will be set at the very top of the agenda of thought on the condition of Israel.

The answer of the sages of the Mishnah links the will of man to the processes of the sanctification of Israel. The message is that what the Israelite wills governs what is holy and determines what is not. The world of nature is neutral. The will of man decides. Nothing, intrinsically, by its nature, is either holy or unclean. The Israelite's purpose determines.

Man is at the center of creation, the head of all creatures upon earth, corresponding to God in Heaven, in whose image man is made. The way in which the Mishnah makes this simple and fundamental statement is to impute power to man to inaugurate and initiate those corresponding processes, sanctification and uncleanness, which play so critical a role in the Mishnah's account of reality. The will of man, expressed through the deed of man, is the active power in the world. Will and deed constitute those actors of creation that work upon neutral realms, subject to either sanctification or uncleanness: the Temple and table, the field and family, the altar and hearth, woman, time, space, transactions in the material world and in the world above as well. An object, a substance, a transaction, even a phrase or a sentence is inert but may be made holy, when the interplay of the will and deed of man arouses or generates its potential to be sanctified. Each may be treated as ordinary or (where relevant) made unclean by the neglect of the will and inattentive act of man. Just as the entire system of uncleanness and holiness awaits the intervention of man, which imparts the capacity to become unclean upon what was formerly inert, or which removes the capacity to impart cleanness from what was formerly in its natural and puissant condition, so in the other ranges of reality, man is at the center on earth, just as is God in heaven. Man is counterpart and partner in creation, in that like God he has power over the status and condition of creation, putting everything in its proper place, calling everything by its rightful name.

So, stated briefly, the question taken up by the Mishnah is, What can a man do? And the answer laid down by the Mishnah is, Man through will and deed, is master of this world, the measure of all things. Since when the Mishnah thinks of man, it means the Israelite, who is the subject and actor of its system, the statement is clear. This man is Israel, who can do what he wills. In the aftermath of the two wars, the message of the Mishnah cannot have proved more pertinent—or poignant and tragic.

The centrality of the human will emerges when we consider how Mishnah answers the questions it chooses to ask. The Mishnah, like any law code, presents an exercise in sorting things out, exploring the limits of conflict and the range of consensus. The one thing which the Mishnah's framers predictably want to know concerns what falls between two established categories or rules, the gray area of the law, the excluded middle among entities, whether persons, places, or things. This obsession with the liminal or marginal comes to its climax and fulfillment in the remarkably wide-ranging inquiry into the nature of mixtures, whether these are mixtures of substances in a concrete framework or of principles and rules in an abstract one. So the question is fully phrased by both the style of the Mishnaic discourse and its rhetoric. It then is fully answered. The question of how we know what something is, the way in which we assign to its proper frame and category what crosses the lines between categories, is settled by what the Israelite man wants, thinks, hopes, believes, and how he so acts as to indicate his attitude. With the question properly phrased in the style and mode of Mishnaic thought and discourse, the answer is not difficult to express. What makes the difference, what sets things into their proper category and resolves those gray areas of confusion and conflict formed when simple principles intersect and produce dispute, is man's will; Israel's despair or hope is the definitive and differentiating criterion.

The evidence of the Mishnah points to a Judaism which answers that question simply: Man, like God, makes the world work. If man wills it, nothing is impossible. When man wills it, all things fall subject to that web of intangible status and incorporeal reality, with a right place for all things, each after its kind, all bearing their proper names, described by the simple word "sanctification." The world is inert and neutral. Man by his word and will initiates the processes that force things to find their rightful place on one side or the other of the frontier, the definitive category, holiness.

This will of man is what differentiates. This intention of man has the power of taxonomy. The Mishnah's Judaism is a system built to celebrate that power of man to form intention, willfully to make the world with full deliberation, in entire awareness, through decision and articulated intent. So does the Mishnah assess the condition of Israel, defeated and helpless, yet in its land: without power, yet holy; lacking all focus, in no particular place, certainly without Jerusalem, yet set apart from the nations. This message of the Mishnah clashes with a reality itself cacophonous, full of dissonance and disorder. The evidence of the Mishnah points to a Judaism defiant of the human condition of Israel, triumphant over the circumstance of subjugation and humiliation, thus surpassing all reality. All of this is to be through the act of Israel's own mind and heart.

vii. Beyond Catastrophe, before the End

The intellectuals whose work we have studied exhibit a deep yearning for stability and order. By these terms they mean having things in place, each thing under its rightful name. The way to put things into place and sort them out, as we see, is to will them so. It is hardly surprising that men of mind in the end should recommend that people solve their problems by using their minds and hearts. Nor should we find it puzzling that the sages before us maintain that the intellect disposes of all problems. What I find strange is a different fact. The Mishnah recommends as a solution to catastrophic change the construction of a world without end, as though such thing were possible. The one thing the sages of the Mishnah had to know—since the Hebrew Scriptures told them so—was that, until the end comes, the end has not come. History stretched backward by their count, for perhaps fourteen or fifteen hundred years. We have to ask ourselves why, then, the Mishnah's philosophers should have reached the conclusion they did. How could they suppose that the nonhistorical and ahistorical world of being laid forth in their book would last?

If we set ourselves down in their day and place, the first thing we notice is how the sages have laid emphasis upon those things, yet within Israel's realm of rule, in which the sacred still endured. Israel remained in the Holy Land The life of the villages went on. The land was farmed, the crops exchanged or sold, the priesthood continued to observe its genealogical rules and eat its holy rations. True, the Temple was no more, the city closed off from Israel. But plans could be made, rules could be studied, the moment defied, eternity affirmed. Accordingly, the Mishnah focused upon what had survived out of a lost past, what could be reconstructed in a better time to come. It described a world set apart from history, because it spoke of an interim between history and eternity, a time after, an age before. The surpassing act of mind and will before us in this book represented a judgment on what could be done even now, when all was lost. For all was not lost. The survivors lived. What a man could do was affirm, believe, endure. What Israel yet possessed was its will. And the will made all the difference.

True, what we see is the prescription for a life of denial of life, as the sages instructed Israel to undertake a grand pretense. Yet no one could have imagined nothing had happened. If the Mishnah's pages lack reference to the age at hand, except for some minor and casual allusions, it is because the sages had no need to speak of context and constituency: defeated Israel, yet left in the holy land, Israel holy as before. What required attention was the state of mind and soul of the holy people in its holy land. Nothing really changed, so long as the holy people was in its holy land. The Mishnah's message was that the glory and the power of Israel depended, as it always had, on the will and heart of Israel. These were what defeat had changed. When we consider the issue as it had been framed by Jeremiah and Ezekiel, IV Ezra and Paul, we find that the Mishnah is so framed as to answer directly and without pretense precisely the question raised in the ages of catastrophe and cataclysm that had gone before. Jeremiah's message about the new covenant, written in the heart, and IV Ezra's and Paul's profound reflections on the incongruity between the will to do the right thing but the inability to do what one wills, here find counterpart and completion. You can indeed do the good that you will, if you will it hard enough. The reason is that, within the mind and heart of Israel, lies the ultimate power over nature and the supernatural alike. Israel's intention decides whatever really matters: what is common, what is holy, what is inert, what is to be changed, who sanctifies.

Beyond catastrophe, Israel once more asks, What can we have done? What can we do now? The Mishnah's sages reply, It all depends upon what you want. You decide your own destiny, in accord with the rule of God. If Israel wills what is right, Israel can do what is right. For sanctification is an act of will. And the sanctification of Israel, the holy people, will mark the end of the age of catastrophe, the beginning of the world beyond time: the present, here and now, if you will it.

Index